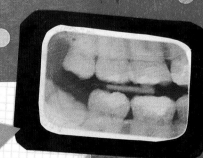

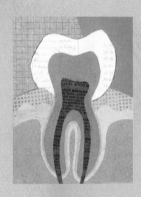

Text copyright © 2008 by Harriet Ziefert

Illustrations copyright © 2008 by Liz Murphy

All rights reserved / CIP Data is available.

Published in the United States 2008 by

Blue Apple Books, 515 Valley Street, Maplewood, N.J. 07040

www.blueapplebooks.com

Distributed in the U.S. by Chronicle Books

First Edition

Printed in China

ISBN: 978-1-934706-31-2

2 4 6 8 10 9 7 5 3 1

Harriet Ziefert

A B C

DENTIST

Liz Murphy

Blue Apple Books

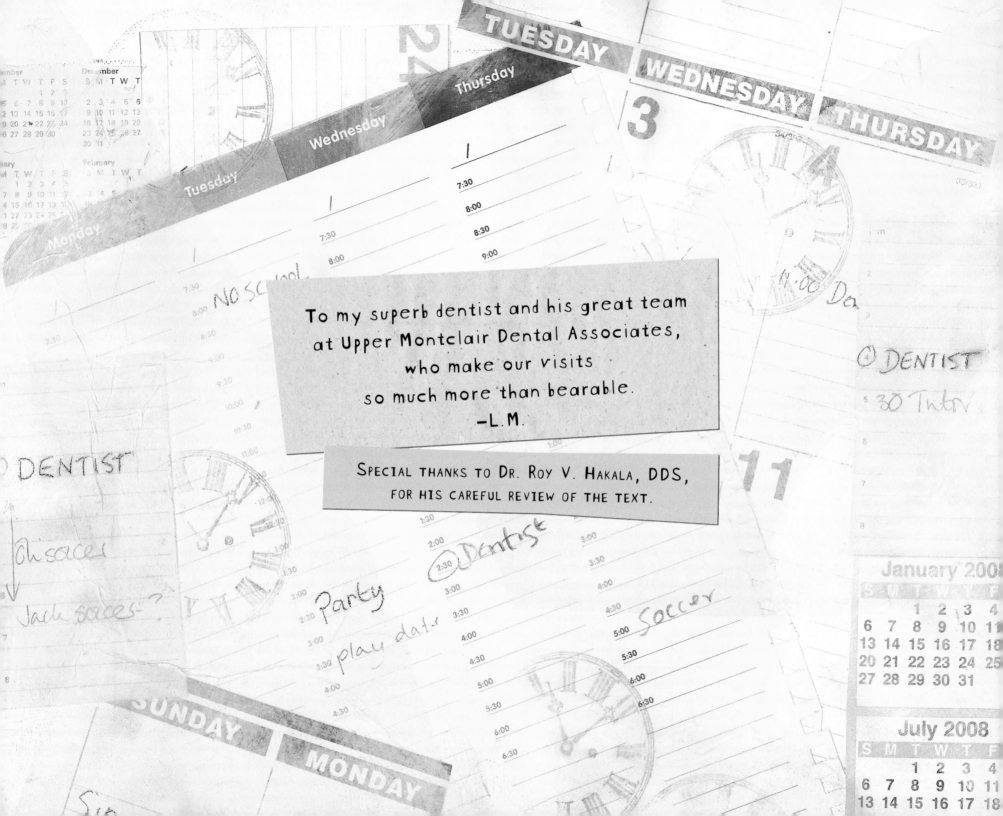

To my superb dentist and his great team
at Upper Montclair Dental Associates,
who make our visits
so much more than bearable.
—L.M.

SPECIAL THANKS TO DR. ROY V. HAKALA, DDS,
FOR HIS CAREFUL REVIEW OF THE TEXT.

APPOINTMENT

It's important to have an **appointment** with the dentist at least once every year, and sometimes twice, if your dentist recommends it.

BIB

You'll need a **bib** at your appointment, so that you don't dribble on your clothes and so the dentist doesn't get your shirt dirty.

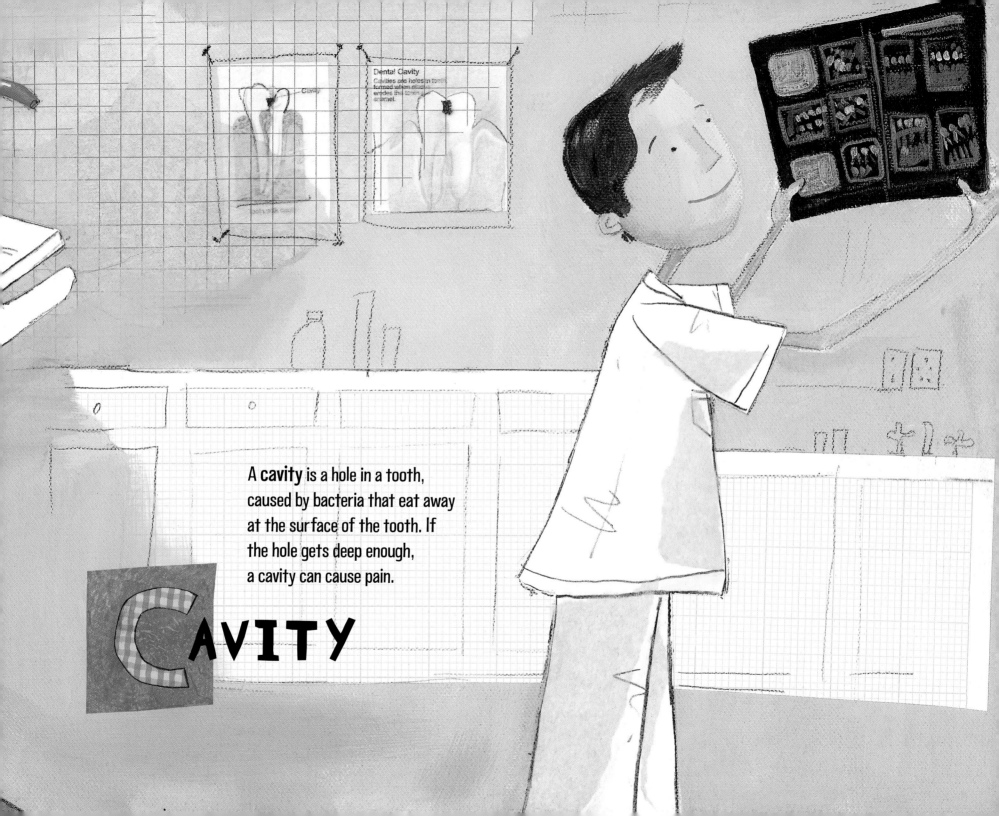

A **cavity** is a hole in a tooth, caused by bacteria that eat away at the surface of the tooth. If the hole gets deep enough, a cavity can cause pain.

CAVITY

Dental Cavity
Cavities are holes in tooth formed when plaque erodes the tooth enamel.

Cavity

DENTAL CHAIR

The chair you sit in at the dentist's office can lean back and go up or down, so that the dentist can get a good look in your mouth.

EXAMINATION

With a bright light, an explorer, and a mirror, the dentist **examines** the surface of the tooth to make sure it's healthy.

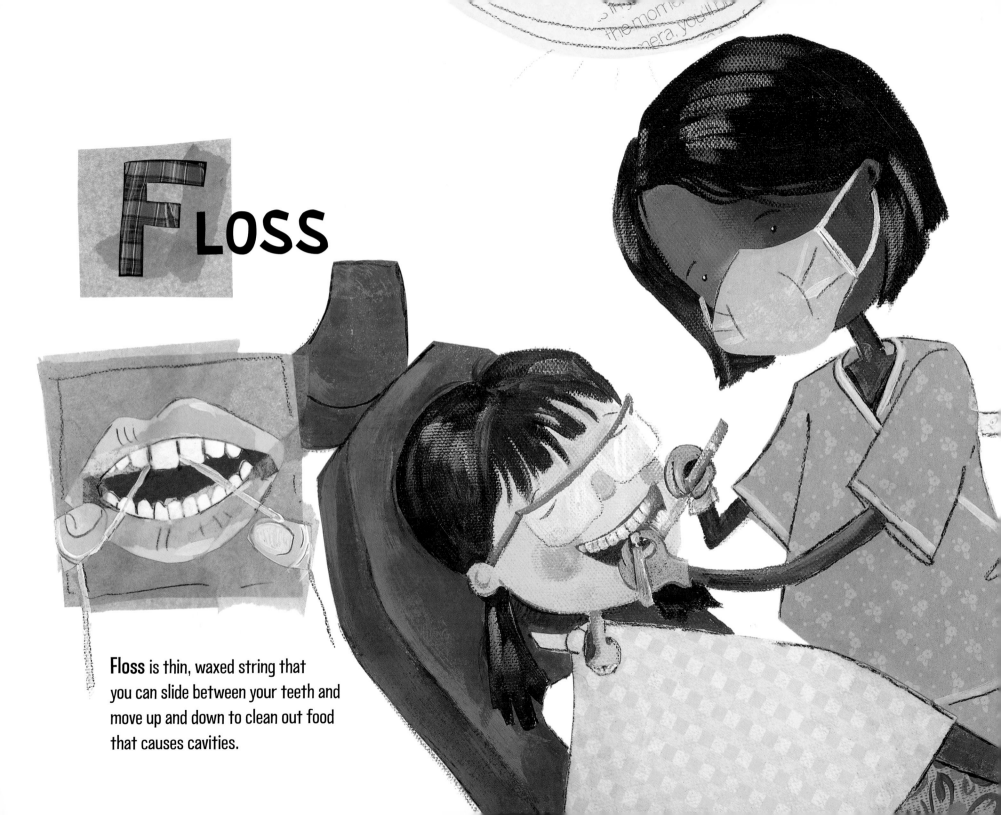

FLOSS

Floss is thin, waxed string that you can slide between your teeth and move up and down to clean out food that causes cavities.

Gums are the smooth pink tissue that protects the roots of the teeth. They may bleed if you do not keep your teeth clean.

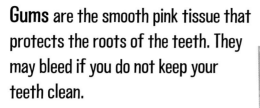

GUMS

HYGIENIST

A **hygienist** cleans your teeth so they stay healthy.

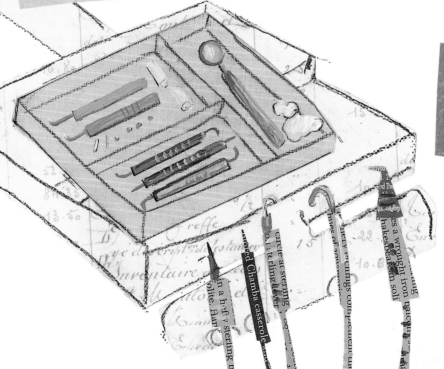

INSTRUMENTS

The dentist uses many **instruments**, and usually begins an examination with an explorer and a mirror.

Jaw

Every person has an upper **jaw** and a lower jaw. The lower jaw is hinged so you can open your mouth. The teeth fit into special holes, called sockets, in the jawbone.

floss

two pieces

toothpaste

KIT

Every person should have a **kit** that holds everything they need for cleaning their teeth: toothpaste, toothbrush, and dental floss.

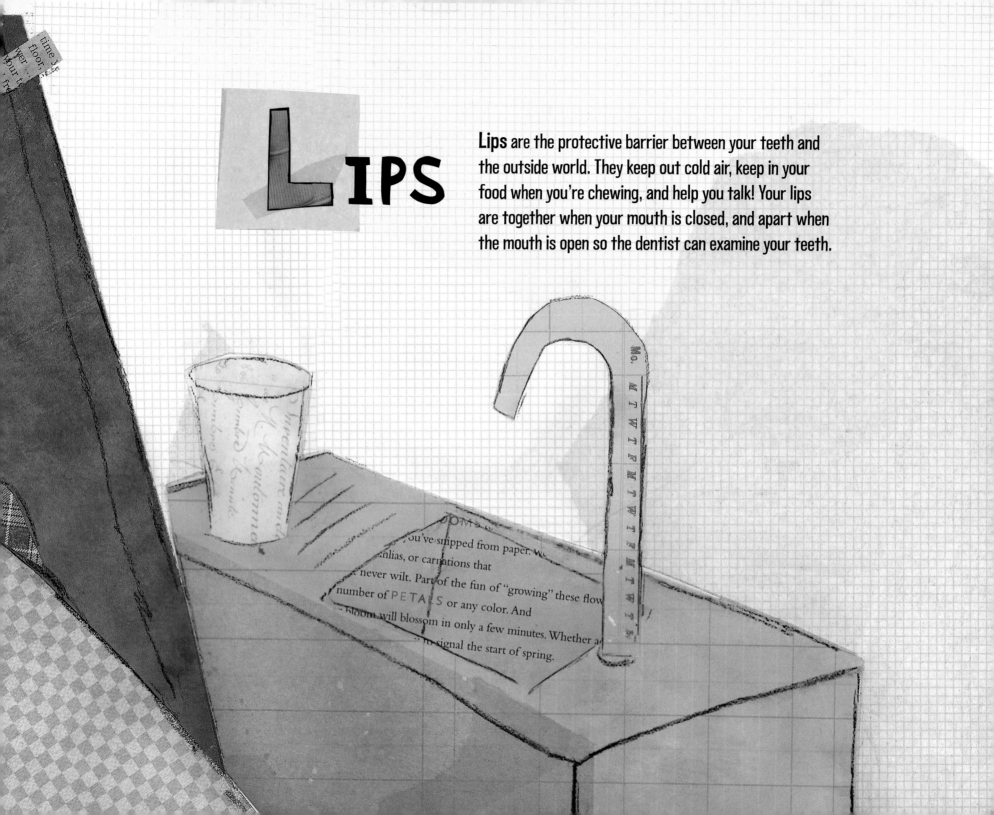

LIPS

Lips are the protective barrier between your teeth and the outside world. They keep out cold air, keep in your food when you're chewing, and help you talk! Your lips are together when your mouth is closed, and apart when the mouth is open so the dentist can examine your teeth.

Mouthwash

A special liquid to swish around in your mouth and gargle with. **Mouthwash** makes your breath smell better and kills germs that cause plaque.

mouth wash

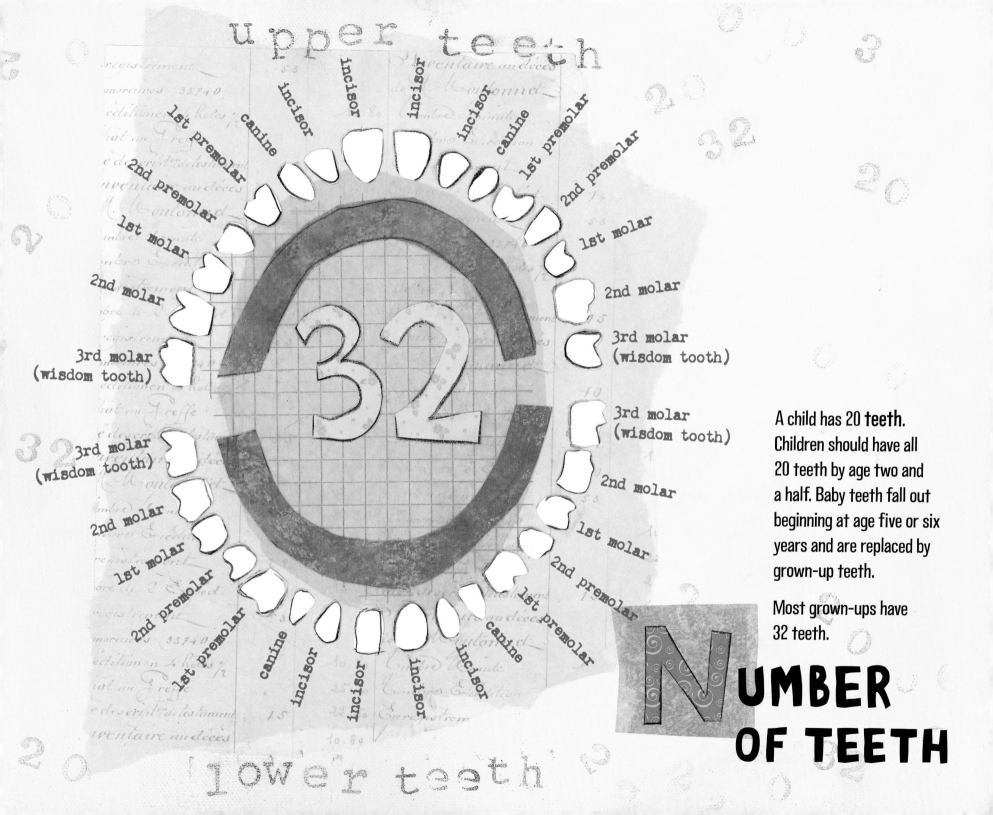

upper teeth

incisor
incisor
incisor
incisor
canine
canine
1st premolar
1st premolar
2nd premolar
2nd premolar
1st molar
1st molar
2nd molar
2nd molar
3rd molar
(wisdom tooth)
3rd molar
(wisdom tooth)

32

3rd molar
(wisdom tooth)
3rd molar
(wisdom tooth)
2nd molar
2nd molar
1st molar
1st molar
2nd premolar
2nd premolar
1st premolar
1st premolar
canine
canine
incisor
incisor
incisor
incisor

lower teeth

A child has 20 **teeth.**
Children should have all
20 teeth by age two and
a half. Baby teeth fall out
beginning at age five or six
years and are replaced by
grown-up teeth.

Most grown-ups have
32 teeth.

NUMBER OF TEETH

ORTHODONTIST

A dentist who specializes in straightening crooked teeth is an **Orthodontist**.

He figures out what to do if a child's jaw is too crowded and may recommend braces, a removable appliance, or removing some baby teeth to make room for grown-up teeth.

PLAQUE

Plaque is an almost invisible white, sticky coating on teeth that is caused by eating sugar and sticky foods. If not cleaned off, plaque can cause cavities and gum disease.

QUESTIONS

Patient: **"Will it hurt?"**

Dentist: "It doesn't have to hurt. If what I'm going to do might hurt, I will inject some medicine so you won't feel it."

Patient: **"Will it bleed?"**

Dentist: "It may bleed a little, but not enough to do you any harm."

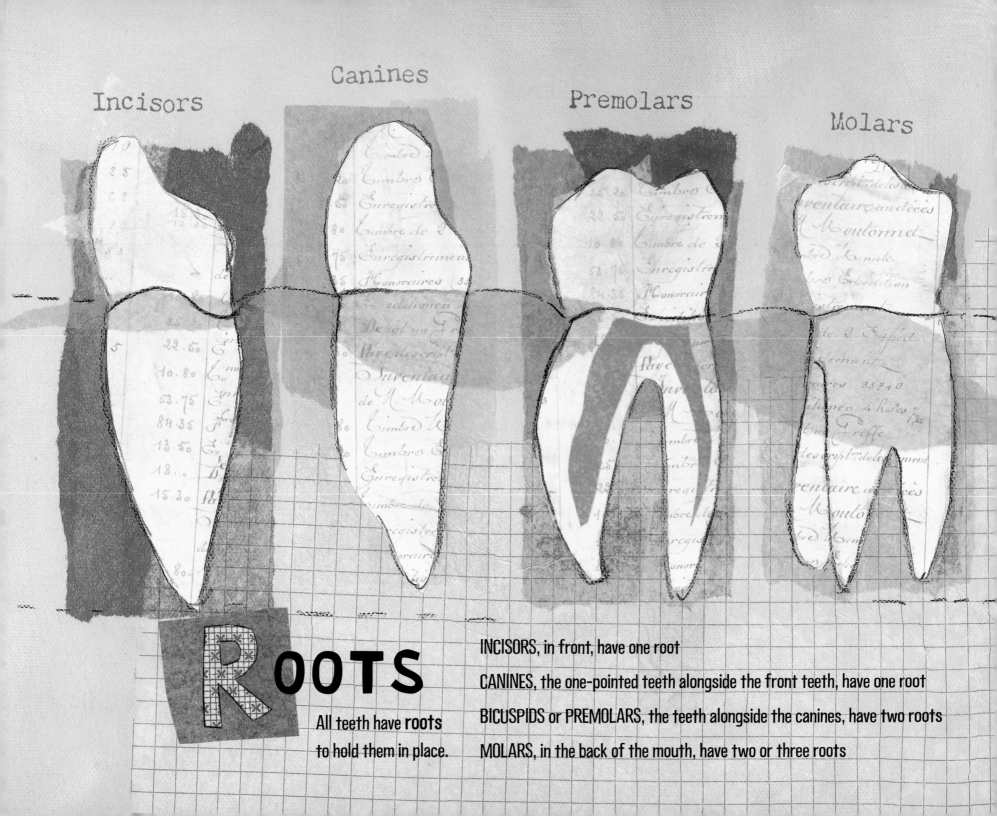

Incisors

Canines

Premolars

Molars

Roots

All teeth have **roots** to hold them in place.

INCISORS, in front, have one root

CANINES, the one-pointed teeth alongside the front teeth, have one root

BICUSPIDS or PREMOLARS, the teeth alongside the canines, have two roots

MOLARS, in the back of the mouth, have two or three roots

SALIVA

The watery, tasteless liquid that's in everyone's mouth. **Saliva** lubricates chewed food, keeps the mouth moist, and helps begin the digestion of starchy food.

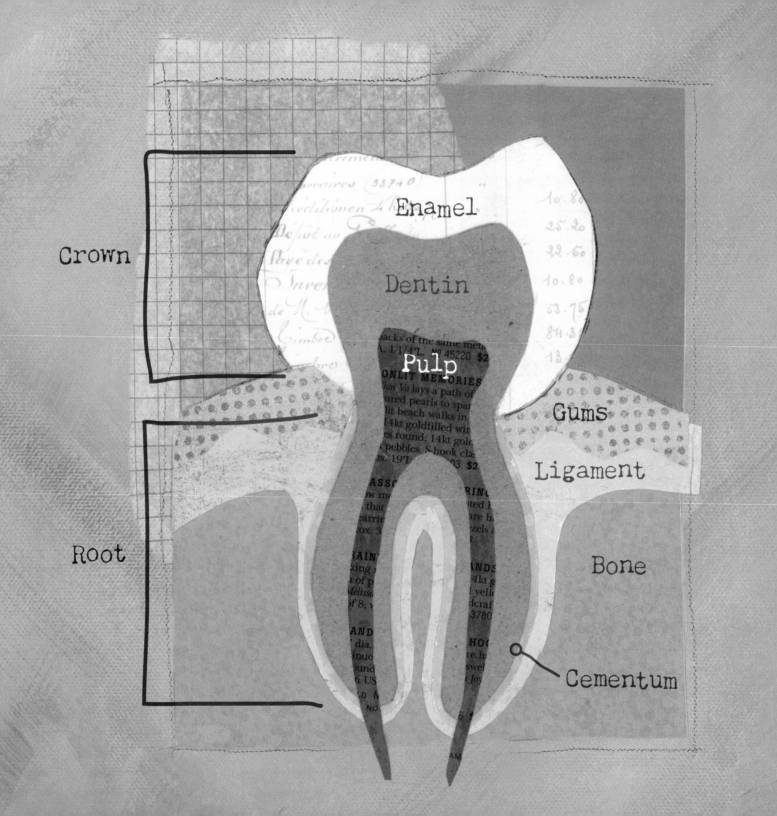

TEETH

Teeth are the hardest parts of a person's body, even harder than bones. They are made up of these parts:

CROWN The part of a tooth that isn't inside the gums—all of the tooth that you can see

ENAMEL The thin, white substance that covers each tooth

DENTIN The hard, dense substance that makes up most of the tooth

PULP The soft tissue inside the dentin, the part of your tooth that feels hot and cold

ROOT The part of the tooth that's underneath the gums

CEMENTUM A layer of bony tissue between the dentin and the gum

GUMS The smooth skin that surrounds your teeth

BONE Your jaw bone, which supports your teeth and gums

LIGAMENT Tissue that holds your teeth in place and connects them to your gums and bone

ULCER

An **Ulcer** is a painful sore on the gums, lips, palate, or tongue, caused by trauma or germs. It's also called a canker sore.

VITAMINS

Teeth and gums need **vitamins** to stay healthy.
There are many different vitamins.
Vitamin D, which comes from milk, helps make teeth strong.
Vitamin C, which is in orange juice, fights bacteria that can cause gum disease and loosening of the teeth.

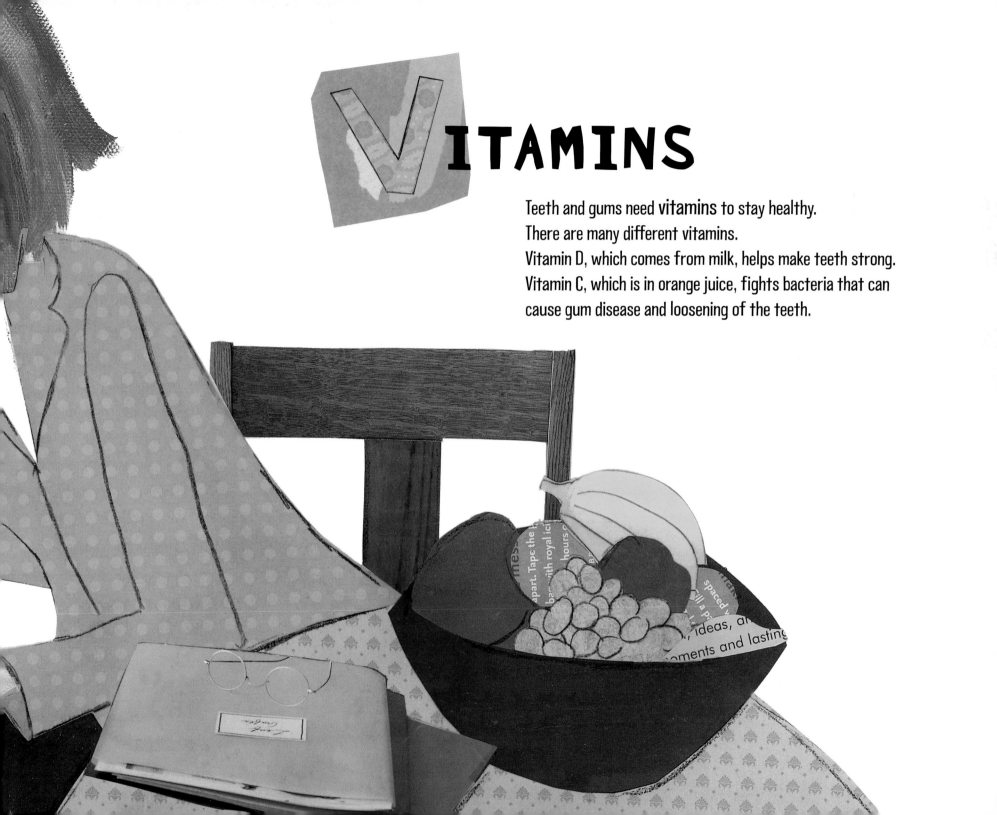

WAD OF COTTON

The dentist puts wads or rolls of **cotton** in your mouth when working to dry up saliva, or to stop bleeding.

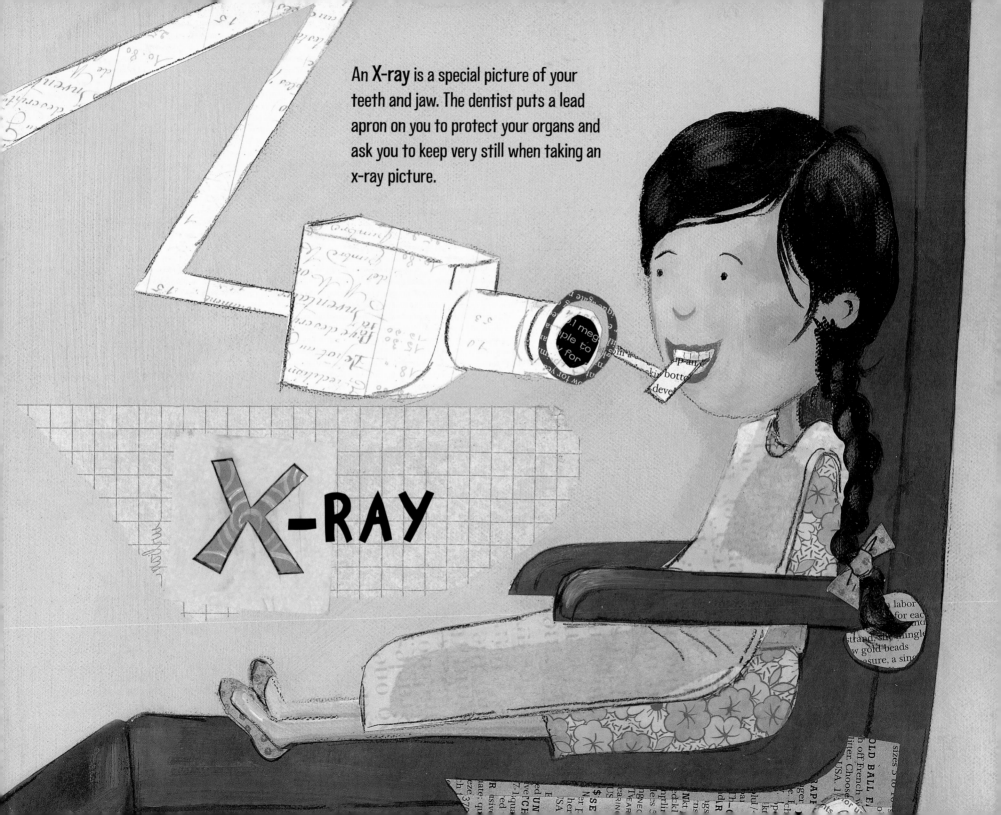

An **X-ray** is a special picture of your teeth and jaw. The dentist puts a lead apron on you to protect your organs and ask you to keep very still when taking an x-ray picture.

X-RAY

Yellow

Teeth that are not clean have a yellow or green coating on the surface. This "dirt" contains bacteria and often makes your breath smell bad. Teeth must be cleaned every day so bacteria doesn't stick to the teeth and cause cavities or gum disease.

After an appointment at the dentist, your teeth are A **ZILLION TIMES CLEANER!**